Let's Explore

What size is it?

by Henry Pluckrose

W

FRANKLIN WATTS
NEW YORK • LONDON • SYDNEY

Author's note

This book is one of a series which has been designed to encourage young readers to think about the everyday concepts that form part of their world. The text and photographs complement each other, and both elements combine to provide starting points for discussion. Although each book is complete in itself, each title links closely with others in the set, so presenting an ideal platform for learning.

I have consciously avoided 'writing down' to my readers. Young children like to know the 'real' words for things, and are better able to express themselves when they can use correct terms with confidence.

Young children learn from the experiences they share with adults around them. The child offers his or her ideas which are then developed and extended through the adult. The books in this series are a means for the child and adult to share informal talk, photographs and text, and the ideas which accompany them.

One particular element merits comment. Information books are also reading books. Like a successful story book, an effective information book will be turned to again and again. As children develop, their appreciation of the significance of fact develops too. The young child who asks 'What is a number?' may subsequently and more provocatively ask, 'What is the biggest number in the world?' Thoughts take time to generate. Hopefully books like those in this series provide the momentum for this.

Henry Pluckrose

Contents

We measure things to find out
what size they are.
There are many different
words to describe size:
big, small, long,
short, narrow, wide.
What other words
can you think of?

These boxes are different sizes.
The red box is bigger
than the green box.
The blue box is smaller
than the green box.
Is the yellow box
bigger or smaller
than the green box?

To find out the size of things,
we need to compare them
to something else.
How big do you think
the mouse is?
How can you tell?

These pencils are different lengths.

Which pencil is the longest?

Which pencil is the shortest?

Which two pencils are the same size?

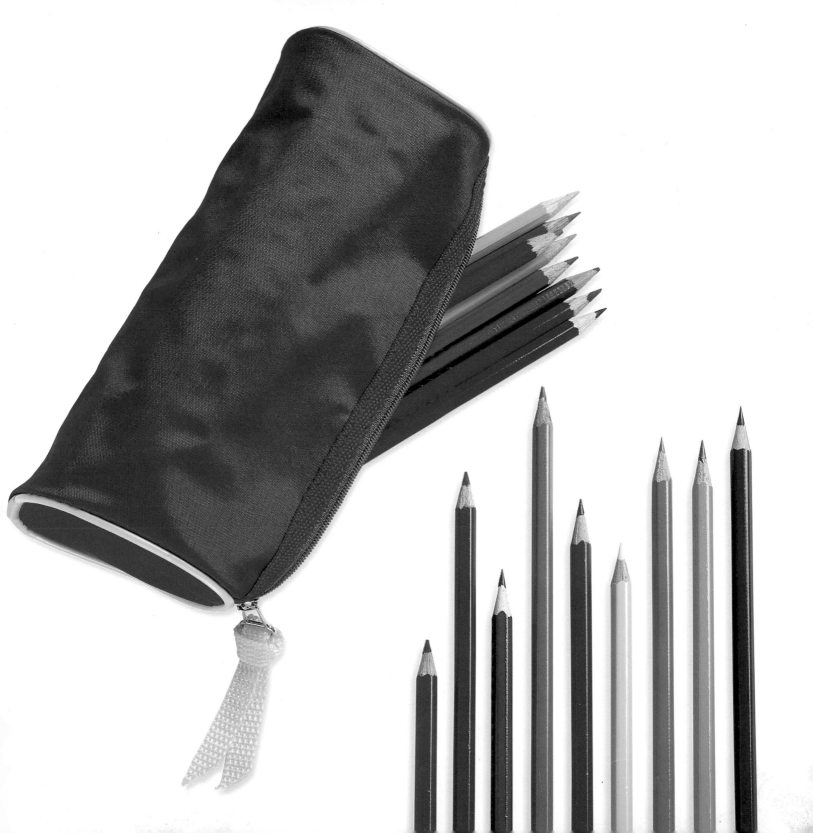

Sometimes we use a ruler to measure.
This ruler is marked with centimetres.

Centimetres are always the same length. How many centimetres long is this caterpillar?

Jessica's height is being measured
by the nurse.
The nurse measures
how tall Jessica is,
from the soles of her feet
to the top of her head.
How tall are you?

There are 100 centimetres in one metre.

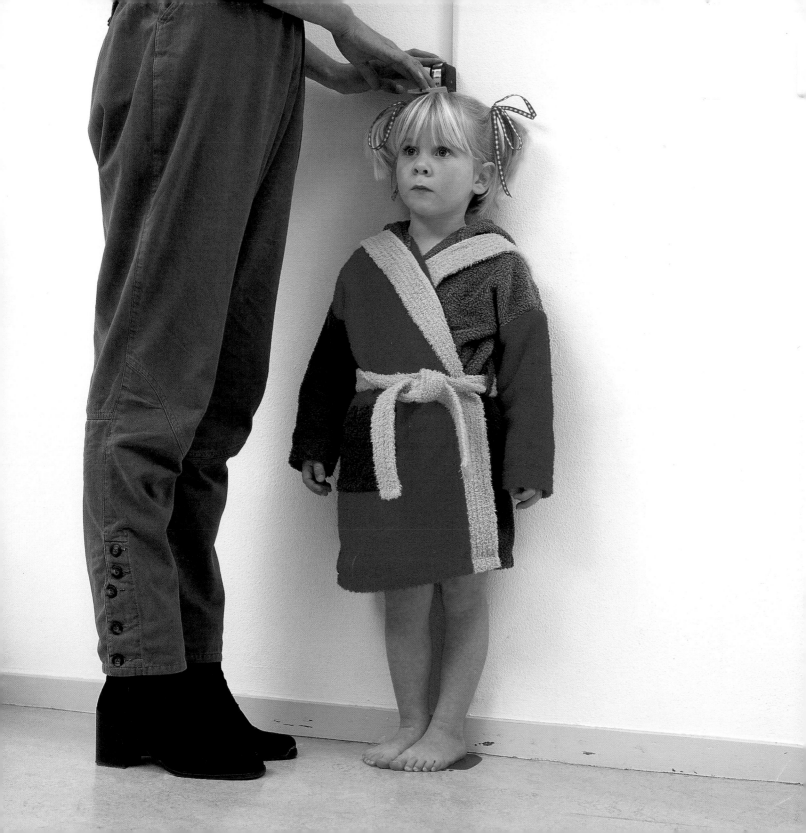

Sometimes we measure things
by their weight.
Letters are weighed
before they are posted.
Each letter is very light.
Lots of letters in the postman's
bag make it
very heavy.

The ball and the balloon
are almost the same size.
Do you think they
weigh the same?

19

To find out what something weighs, we can use scales.
We measure weight in grams and kilograms.
James is weighing the flour on the kitchen scales.
It weighs 100 grams.

Everything has a weight.
These scales are made
especially to weigh people.
Things which are heavy
are measured in kilograms.
How heavy are you?

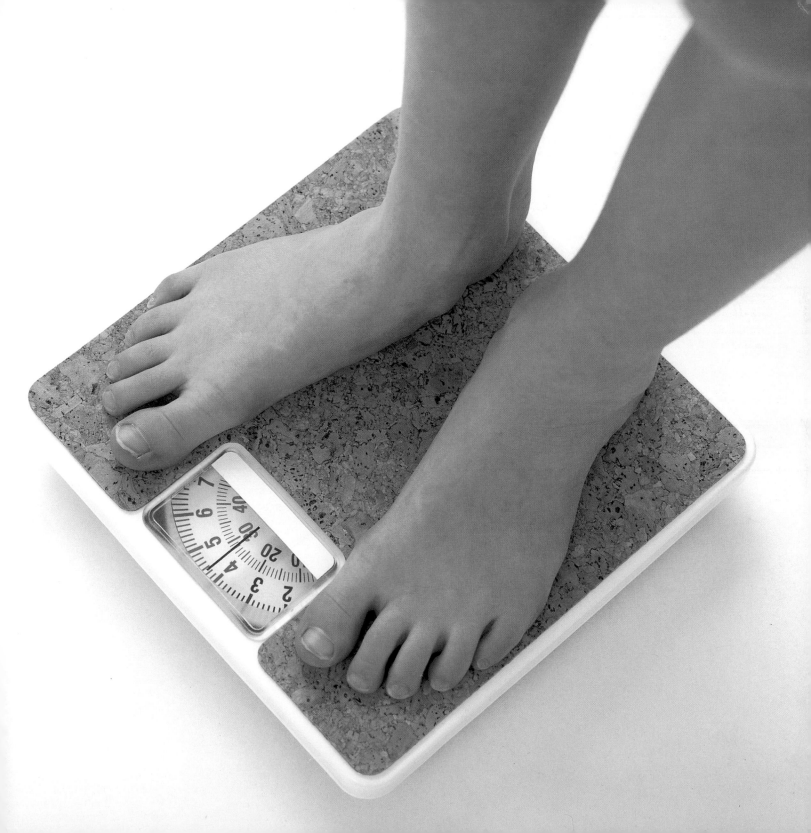

These two bottles are full of water.
We measure water and other liquids
in millilitres and litres.
These two bottles
are different in shape,
but each bottle holds
the same quantity of water.

This bucket can hold
ten litres of water.
The amount it can hold
is called its capacity.
Even when the bucket is empty,
it still has the same capacity.

27

Megan is going away on holiday.
Do you think the suitcase
will hold all her things?
What will she have
to leave behind?

We can measure things
in many ways.
Take this road tanker,
for example ...

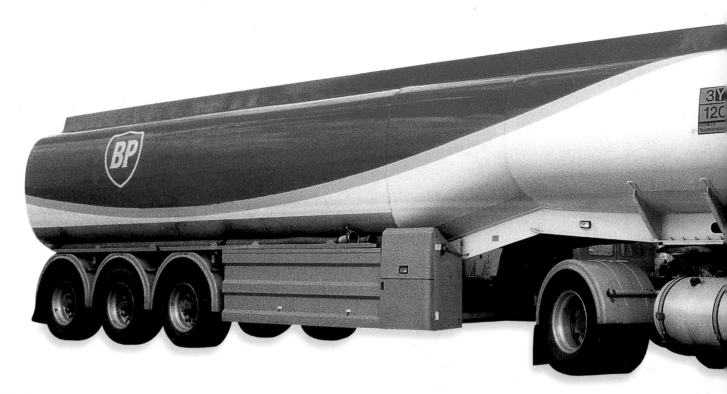

We can measure its capacity.
We can measure its weight.
We can measure its length,
height and breadth.
How many
ways can you
be measured?

Index

First published in 1999 by
Franklin Watts
96 Leonard Street
London
EC2A 4XD

Franklin Watts Australia
14 Mars Road
Lane Cove
NSW 2066

Copyright © Franklin Watts 1999

ISBN 0 7496 3573 8

Dewey Decimal
Classification Number 516

A CIP catalogue record for this book is
available from the British Library

Series editor: Louise John
Series designer: Jason Anscomb
Series consultant: Peter Patilla

Printed in Hong Kong

Picture Credits:
Steve Shott Photography pp. cover and title
page, 4, 6, 11, 12/13, 19, 21, 22, 25, 27, 28,
30/31; Chris Honeywell p. 16; Bubbles p. 15
(Frans Rombout); Image Bank p. 9 (Bob
Elsdale).

With thanks to our models:
Ashton Burns, Megan Eedle, Hattie
Hundertmark, Thaddeus Jeffries, Wilf
Kimberley, Alice Snedden.